A Song in Her Heart

written by

Zidina Hoyte

ISBN -978-1-990420-23-8

Copyright © 2025 by Zidina Hoyte

All rights reserved.

Designed and published by Labworks Publishing Inc.

Zora is the sweetest little girl, and she just *Loves* to sing.

In the morning, she rejoices with a song as she greets the day.

She hums as she eats her favourite breakfast cereal.

She even sings as she strolls along on her way to school.
"Good day, Mr. and Mrs. Thompson," she shouts.
"Always singing, that sweet Zora," says Mrs. Thompson.

One afternoon, on her way to math class, Zora notices a poster for the school talent show. She is filled with excitement and so nervous at the very same time.

Zora has a song in her heart that she wants to share, but she cannot help but wonder.

"Can I really do this?"

"What if I start on the wrong key?"

"What if I forget the words?"

"OR EVEN WORSE, WHAT IF EVERYONE LAUGHS AT ME?" HA-HA!

While her math teacher is busy writing equations on the board, all Zora could think about is the talent show.

When Zora gets home, she quickly finishes up her homework and then helps her brother set the table for dinner.

Dad says grace, and everyone digs in. Zora, however, stares blankly at her favourite dish, spaghetti and meatballs.

"How was your day?" Dad asks. "It was okay", Zora answers, wondering if she should share about the school talent show.

Zora is playing around with her food, which she normally would have devoured by now.

"How about you, Zach?" Dad asks Zora's younger brother. "My day was great! Zora, did you know that although our sun is the biggest thing in our solar system, compared to other stars in the galaxy, it is only medium-sized? The biggest star discovered so far is called the UY Scuti!" says Zach. Zora zones out as Zach rambles on about space facts.

After dinner, Zora helps her mom clean up and everyone settles down for the night.

As Zora listens to her favourite bedtime playlist, her mom comes in to kiss her goodnight. She can tell that something is still on her mind.

"Zora, is everything alright? You barely said a word all evening and hardly touched your supper. You know you can always talk to me."

"Well…" Zora begins, "I saw a talent show poster in school today and I really want to sing but I just don't know. I feel so nervous. What if I mess up? What if no one thinks I sound good?"

"Come here, sweetheart", Mom says.
"I know that singing in front of a lot of people can feel a bit scary. It's normal to have all these thoughts racing through your mind. We must not allow our fears of making mistakes or not being good enough to stop us from trying. Just do your best."
"Okay, Mommy, I will," Zora says, smiling.

The next day, Zora confidently puts her name on the sign-up list. She rehearses every day at home and at school.

Finally, it is the night before the big show. As Zora settles into bed, the nervous feeling comes back. "Mom, I'm still really nervous about the show," she says quietly.

"I know Zora, but you've got a beautiful song in your heart and you should share it with the world. Remember, just do your best and that's all that matters. You're going to do great!"

The next day, the whole family is ready to see Zora sing in the talent show.
They grab their seats in the auditorium and excitedly search the program for her name.

At last, Zora walks onto centre stage with courage and sings her heart out.

When she finishes, she is so happy to see everyone standing and cheering for her. She takes a big bow. She did it!

After the show, her family is waiting in the hallway
to congratulate her. She hurries over to them,
and they embrace one another.
"Thank you for believing in me! I'm so happy I chose to be brave."
"You did an amazing job, sweet Zora! We're so proud of you."

A CONFIDENCE BOOSTING ACTIVITY

Do you ever feel nervous or afraid to try something new? That's okay—even the bravest people feel that way sometimes!

Here are a few things you can do to help yourself feel BRAVE.

1. **TAKE A FEW DEEP BREATHS**
2. **FOCUS YOUR THOUGHTS ON SOMETHING POSITIVE**
3. **TALK TO SOMEONE YOU TRUST**
4. **REMIND YOURSELF – "MY BEST IS MORE THAN ENOUGH."**
5. **KNOW THIS – YOU ARE LOVED, AND YOU ARE CAPABLE OF AMAZING THINGS.**

www.ingramcontent.com/pod-product-compliance
Lightning Source LLC
Chambersburg PA
CBHW042129040426
42450CB00002B/122